Moving Things

Thousands of years ago
there were no bulldozers,
tractors, trucks, or cranes.
When people had to move heavy loads,
they pushed, pulled, lifted, and carried.
It was hard work.
But people discovered ways
to make hard work easier.
They invented machines.

Levers Are Machines

Cave dwellers discovered they could move
large rocks more easily by using a branch
as a lever. At night, the cave dwellers
would often lever a large rock to the
cave entrance to protect themselves
from prowling wild animals.

5

"Give me a lever
and a place to stand
and I will move the world,"
said the Greek inventor, Archimedes.
(Perhaps he could have, too,
if he had found the right lever!)
Since the days of the cave dwellers,
levers have made work easier for everyone.
Levers are machines.

"Give me a lever . . . I will move the world," said Archimedes.

Levers today.

7

Rollers Are Machines

Even with levers,
the cave dwellers found it hard to move
heavy flat rocks.
Round rocks were easier to move,
because they could be rolled.
People since that time have found
round things easier to move.
And they discovered it was easier to move loads
on round things.

Building the pyramids.

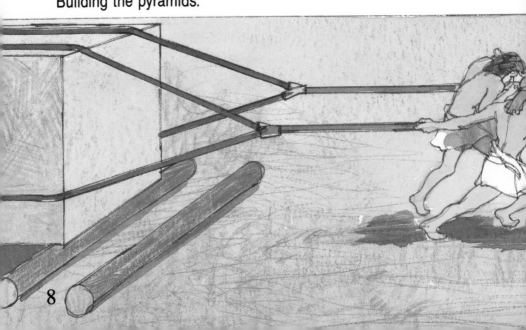

8

Tree trunks could be used as rollers
to move heavy loads.
They made hard work much easier!
The Egyptians used levers and rollers
to move enormous blocks of stone
to build the pyramids.
The pyramids could not have been built
without levers or rollers.

Ramps Are Machines

The pyramids would not have been built at all
without people discovering another machine.
The pyramids were able to be
built because the Egyptians used ramps.
Ramps are machines called inclined planes.
Ramps are used everywhere today.
Ramps are machines.

The Egyptians used ramps.

Ramps today.

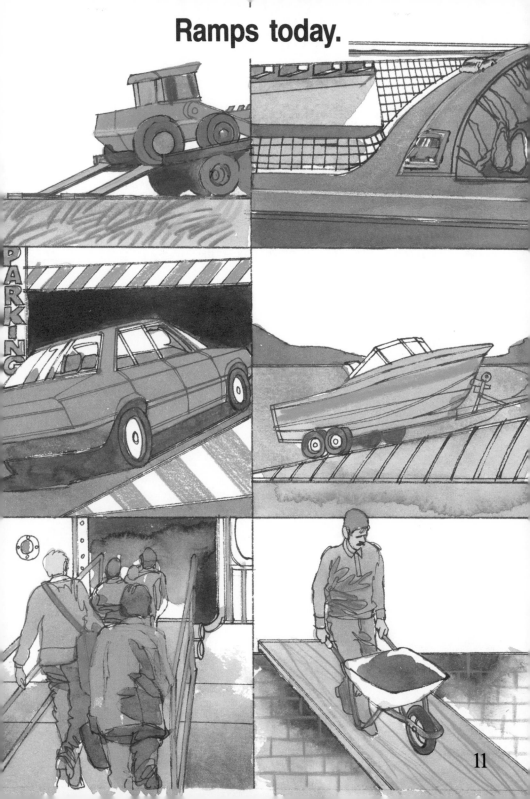

Screws Are Machines

Archimedes, the Greek inventor,
didn't just think about
moving the world with a lever.
He thought about inclined planes, too.
And because Archimedes was a genius,
he thought about a special use
for an inclined plane.
He invented the screw.
A screw is just an inclined plane
going around and around.

Screws are inclined planes.

Archimedes' screw.

Screws today.

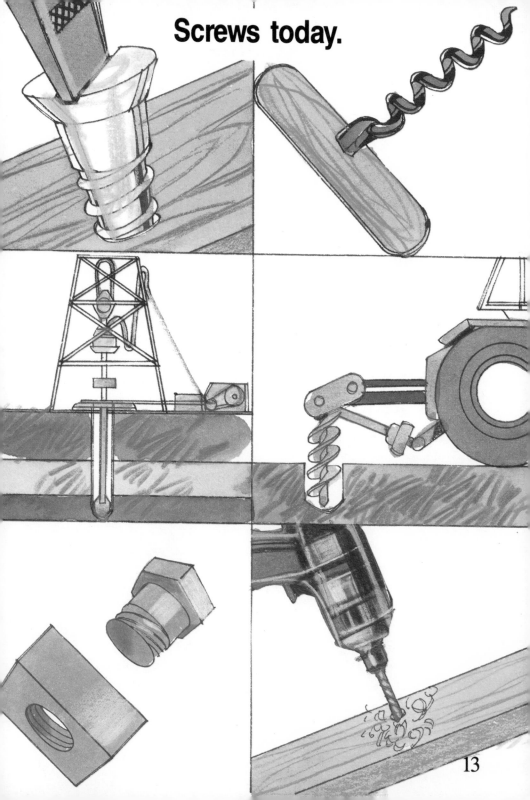

Wedges Are Machines

Many people in past times used wedges.
Wedges are also machines.
At first, people probably used
wedge-shaped rocks they found
to skin animals, cut meat, and shape wood
and bone.
But later they discovered
they could make wedges themselves,
by chipping rocks into the shapes they wanted.
Then they could make tools like axes –
which are wedges with a handle.
Wedges are still important today.
Wedges are machines.

People made wedges by chipping rocks into the shape they wanted.

Wedges today.

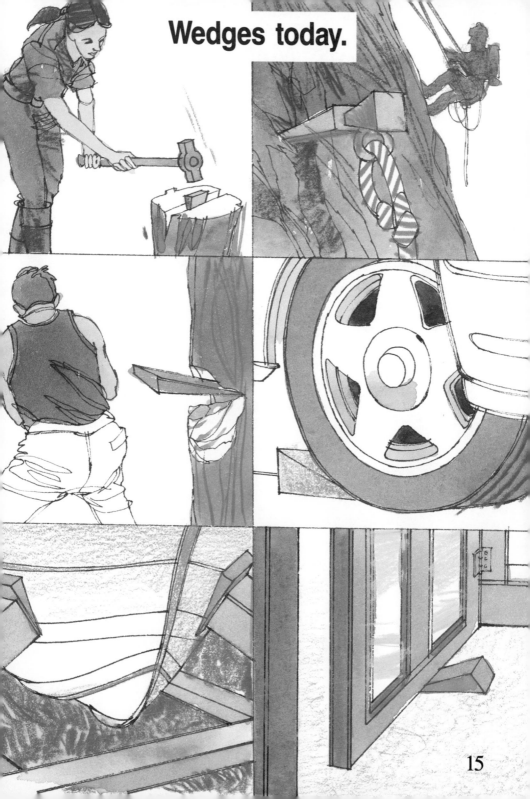

Wheels Are Machines

One of the most important machines
people ever invented is the wheel.
Wheels are machines like rollers.
Wheels are short rollers.
People found that if they joined
two short rollers with an axle,
they had a new machine.
This new machine could move heavy loads
more easily.
Wheels are machines.

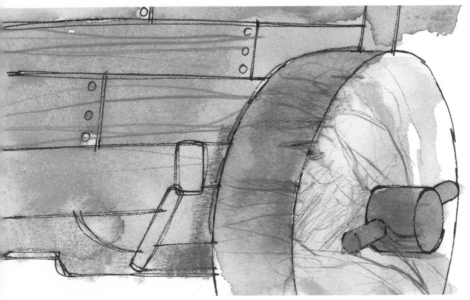

An early wheel.

17

Today, wheels are used in many ways.
Without them, the world would come to a stop!
Cars would stop!
Trains would stop!
Airplanes would not fly!
People would find it hard to lift heavy loads
without pulleys
or winch a boat out of the sea
without gear wheels.

Using wheels in a pulley.

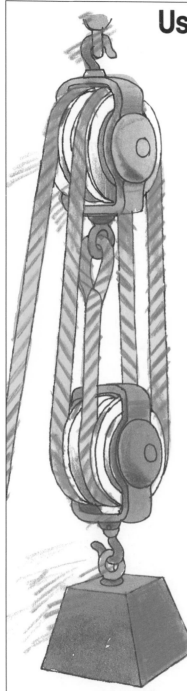

Lifting an engine.

Winching a boat.

We still use the same machines
that people invented long ago.
When you look at a crane lifting cargo
onto a ship, you can see wheels, levers,
wedges, screws, ramps, and rollers.

When you look at a bicycle, a car,
a bulldozer — any machine at all —
you will find levers, rollers,
ramps (or inclined planes),
wedges, screws, and wheels.
They all help make hard work easy.

Even today, people invent machines
that use levers, screws, wedges,
and inclined planes.
Whatever the machines of the future look like,
they'll have some of these machines
to make them work.